Cripple Creek!

A Quick History
of
The World's Greatest Gold Camp

by
Leland Feitz

Published by
LITTLE LONDON PRESS
716 E. Washington St.
Colorado Springs, Colorado

Library of Congress Catalog Card Number: 67-5178

Seventeenth Printing — 1983

DEDICATED TO

BOB WOMACK

"His discovery started the last of the great gold rushes"

The Womack ranch where Cripple Creek was built.

(Denver Public Library Western Collection)

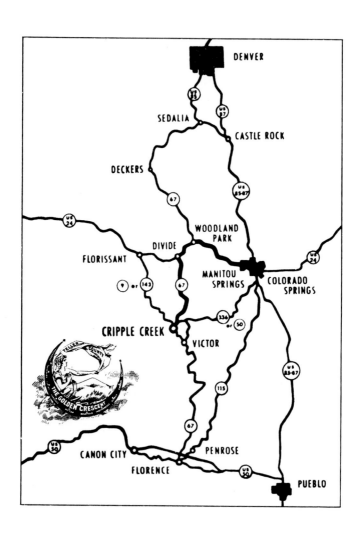

DENVER

SEDALIA

CASTLE ROCK

DECKERS

67

US 85-87

WOODLAND PARK

US 24

DIVIDE

FLORISSANT

MANITOU SPRINGS

COLORADO SPRINGS

US 24

9 or 143

67

CRIPPLE CREEK

136 or 50

VICTOR

115

US 85-87

67

CANON CITY

PENROSE

US 50

FLORENCE

US 50

PUEBLO

Leland Feitz

The author has been a Gold Camp enthusiast since his first trip there in 1945. He has had a summer home in Cripple Creek since 1954, where much of the work on this "quick history" was done.

He has also written "Myers Avenue, A Quick History of Cripple Creek's Red-Light District," "Cripple Creek Railroad," "Victor, A Quick History of Colorado's City of Mines," "Platoro, Mining Camp and Resort Town," "Creede, Colorado Boom Town," "Colorado Trolleys," "The Antlers, Colorado Springs Historic Hotel," "Soapy Smith's Creede," "Ghost Towns of the Cripple Creek District," and "Alamosa, The San Luis Valley's Big City."

The author's Cripple Creek home.

INTRODUCTION

Since our first entrancing view of the distant Sangre de Cristo peaks rimming the far west edge of the bowl encircling Cripple Creek, we have been ardent students of her fascinating history and avid readers of Cripplecreekania anecdotes. This famous gold camp has intrigued artists, writers and historians over the years and many excellent books have been written relating the almost unbelievable tales of Cripple Creek's discovery, development and decline. None, however, has quite satisfied the demand of numerous visitors who feel they have neither the time nor inclination to read history in depth, but still are very much interested in a "short course" in Cripple Creek's colorful and romantic past.

I believe that Leland Feitz has done an admirable job of meeting this need, combining well selected and representative pictures with a short and lively text. A quick perusal of its contents should add much to the visitor's enjoyment of the Cripple Creek district and help him to understand what he sees here. In addition, Mr. Feitz has done a thorough job of research to render his book a valuable addition to a reference collection as well as an excellent souvenir of Cripple Creek.

DOROTHY MACKIN
The Imperial Hotel
Cripple Creek

This was Cripple Creek in November of 1891. Then, it was called Fremont.

Early Bennett Avenue. It became the commercial center of the great gold camp.

GOLD DISCOVERED!

From 1890, when gold was first discovered, until 1961, when the last of the mines stopped operating, over $500,000,000*worth of ore was dug out of the hills of Cripple Creek.

A cowpuncher named Bob Womack made the discovery that started the last of the big gold rushes. After fifteen years of prospecting on the ranch where Cripple Creek now stands, he uncovered real paydirt in a place called Poverty Gulch.

The ore was rich. It assayed at more than $200 a ton. But on a Colorado City drinking spree, Womack sold his claim for a mere $500 and died penniless in 1909.

The land where Womack's first strike was made was homesteaded by his father in 1876. By 1891, it belonged to Horace Bennett and Julias Myers, Denver real estate and cattle men.

Soon after the strike, when people began swarming into the area, Bennett and Myers platted an eighty-acre townsite and began selling lots. The town was officially incorporated in 1892, and it was named Cripple Creek after the stream that meandered through it. The creek had been named earlier by a rancher who had seen a cow fall and cripple herself crossing it.

As other strikes were made in the area, other towns appeared. Victor, the District's second city, was established in 1893, some five miles south and east of Cripple Creek. From the beginning, Victor was called "The City of Mines," for here, on Battle Mountain, the District's largest and richest mines were located.

During the first year following Womack's discovery, the mines of the Cripple Creek field produced about $200,000 worth of gold. The output more than doubled the next year. By 1893, the production was being measured by the millions of dollars.

The camp's population swelled along with its production. Fewer than 500 people lived there at the end of 1891. Twelve months later, the population was 2,500. Then, during 1893, over 10,000 people swarmed into the District. For the next several years, the population continued to grow at the rate of over 500 persons a month.

*Based on values at time of mining

Stage lines ran into Cripple Creek from Divide and Florissant from the year gold was discovered. They loaded and unloaded in front of the Palace Hotel. This is an 1893 scene. (Denver Public Library Western Collection. Photo by H. S. Poley)

Cripple Creek, in 1894, was a town of flimsy pine shacks. This was its main street, Bennett Avenue, three years after Bob Womack discovered gold in Poverty Gulch. Pioneer's Museum, Colorado Springs)

The Crusher, Cripple Creek's first newspaper, appeared in 1891. Nine years later, fifteen papers were being printed in the camp. Cripple Creek, alone, had five daily newspapers (Pioneer's Museum, Colorado Springs)

Victor's main street two years after the founding of "The City of Mines." It grew into the District's second largest community.

Early Myers Avenue, in Cripple Creek, was typically western. This picture of the old "tenderloin" was taken during the winter of 1895-96. (Denver Public Library Western Collection. Photo by H. S. Poley)

Cripple Creek's Bennett Avenue was always the gold camp's "main street." (State Historical Society of Colorado)

THE GREAT FIRES

Both Cripple Creek and Victor were almost totally destroyed by fires during the boom. But even before the ashes had cooled, the two towns began to rebuild, becoming modern cities.

Cripple Creek's first fire broke out on the afternoon of April 25, 1896, in one of the red-light district's dance halls. By dusk of that day, fifteen acres of the town had been leveled. Four days later, a second fire wiped out all that was left except for a few houses in the western part of town.

The two fires destroyed property worth more than $2,000,000. Six lives were lost. Some 5,000 people were left without homes. They were sheltered in huge tent-cities, while Cripple Creek rebuilt with brick.

Three years after the Cripple Creek disasters, Victor was wiped out by fire. Like Cripple Creek's first fire, this one also started in a dance hall. It leveled Victor in only half a day.

Four days after the fire, 100 Victor merchants were back in business in makeshift shacks. On the fifth day, work began on the city's first new brick building.

Bennett Avenue minutes after the start of the first of Cripple Creek's two great fires in April of 1896. (State Historical Society of Colorado)

Cripple Creek was almost totally destroyed by the two fires. Bennett Avenue was completely leveled and 5,000 were left without homes. (Denver Public Library Western Collection. Photo by H. S. Poley)

Before the ashes cooled, Cripple Creek began to rebuild. This is how Bennett Avenue looked during the summer of 1896. The big building under construction at the right is the National Hotel. (Denver Public Library Western Collection. Photo by H. S. Poley)

On August 21, 1899, the city of Victor was leveled by a fire which started in the "999" Dance Hall. Five days later, Victor started to rebuild with brick. (Denver Public Library Western Collection. Photo by H. S. Poley)

Thousands were left homeless by the Victor fire. Many found temporary refuge on the lower slopes of Battle Mountain. (State Historical Society of Colorado)

THE CITIES

By 1900, more than 55,000 people lived in the Cripple Creek District, and Cripple Creek, with its 25,000 population, was the fourth biggest city in Colorado. Victor, with a population of over 18,000, was the state's next city in size. Another eleven towns, with populations ranging from 500 to 3,500, were scattered about the gold camp.

From the start, Cripple Creek was the District's leading commercial center. In 1899, when Teller County was established, Cripple Creek was made the county seat. The stock exchange and half the District's banks were on Bennett Avenue. When the city was its largest, it supported forty brokers, seventy-two lawyers and thirty-nine real estate agents.

Of the District's fifteen newspapers, eight were published in Cripple Creek. Five of them were daily papers. One, *The Colored Tribune*, was published for the big Negro population. Victor had two dailies.

Two-thirds of the District's ninety doctors were located in Cripple Creek. Many of them had their offices in the four-story Fairley & Lampman Block. Both Cripple Creek and Victor had big, modern hospitals, and each city had two undertakers.

If the gold camp had a "main street," it was certainly Cripple Creek's Bennett Avenue. For five long blocks it was lined with every kind of business. There were four department stores, including a May Company, two dance schools, a business college, four book shops, nine photographers and dozens of specialty shops.

Scattered throughout Cripple Creek were forty-nine grocery stores, twenty meat markets, fourteen bakeries and eleven laundries. There were five livery stables and eleven blacksmith shops. Milk was delivered to the homes in the District by eleven different dairies.

Victor's lively business district was about two-thirds as big as Cripple Creek's. The streets there were literally paved with gold, for in the early days, only high-grade ore was shipped to the mills, much of the low-grade ore being used to pave the city's streets.

Both cities had excellent hotels. The District's largest, and one of Colorado's finest, was The National in Cripple Creek. A five-floor building, it opened in 1896, with 150 guest rooms.

Cripple Creek Builds! The large building under construction is the 150 room National Hotel, the largest and finest hotel ever built in the District. To the left of it, the new Gold Mining Stock Exchange Building is taking shape. (Denver Public Library Western Collection)

Bennett Avenue was almost totally rebuilt after the fires of 1896. These new store buildings face on Bennett at the corner of Third Street. The building with the tower housed Cripple Creek's May Co. (Denver Public Library Western Collection)

In addition to the hotels' dining rooms, the two cities had thirty restaurants. A good dinner cost about 35 cents at Delmonico's, The New Yorker, Merchant's Cafe or The Saddle Rock.

Seventy-three of the District's 150 saloons were in Cripple Creek. Most of them were on Myers Avenue, the big town's "sin street." Here, too, were the dance halls, variety theatres, parlour houses and cribs. And this is where the big Grand Opera House stood.

While there were gambling houses galore on Myers Avenue, the big ones were up on Bennett. These included The Branch, Board of Trade, Johnnie Nolan's and The Antlers Club.

Victor, too, had a "tenderloin" with some thirty-five gambling halls and saloons, centering on First Street. Van's Big Gem, The Fortune, Star of the West and The Saratoga were some of the clubs that were open there twenty-four hours every day.

Goldfield, a suburb of Victor, was the District's third largest city and its most attractive residential community. By 1900, there were 3,500 people living there.

Because of its Pinnacle Park, Cameron is one of the best remembered of the small towns. While it was never home to more than a few hundred, it was often the playground of thousands. On Labor Day in 1900, more than 9,000 people paid admission to its amusement park. Spreading over some thirty acres, it had a fine little zoo, dance pavilions, athletic fields, rides, picnic areas and a variety of restaurants.

Altman, elevation 10,620 feet, was then the highest incorporated city in the world. About 1,500 people lived there at the turn-of-the-century.

Just below Altman was the camp town of Independence. It was strung out in a gulch for about half a mile with some 2,000 people living there in 1900.

Elkton, midway between Cripple Creek and Victor, once had a population of about 2,500. Near it was Anaconda, another camp town. Its population reached 1,500 in 1900.

Railroad shops and a big ore reduction mill created a healthy payroll for the town of Gillett. About 1,200 people lived there in 1900. The District's only bank, outside Cripple Creek and Victor, was in Gillett, and a newspaper called *The Forum* was published there.

At the turn of the century, Cripple Creek was Colorado's fourth biggest city. Its population was over 25,000. (Denver Public Library)

Victor, in 1900, had a population of 18,000. It was the fifth largest city in the state.

The big five story National Hotel can be seen behind the City of Cripple Creek Mine. The building to the left of the hotel is the Stock Exchange.

The Gold Coin Mine stood in the heart of downtown Victor. The long building to the right of the mine housed the exclusive Gold Coin Club.

This was Bennett Avenue in 1908. The street car is turning onto Second Street and is heading back to Victor.

Victor's main street was Victor Avenue. This is how it looked in 1900. The Victor Opera House can be seen in the right foreground. (Collection of Fred and Jo Mazzulla)

Second Street in Cripple Creek, between Bennett and Myers. (Denver Public Library Western Collection. Photo by H. S. Poley)

This is how the Hub Store advertised itself on Cripple Creek's streets in the early part of the century.

Goldfield was the District's third largest city. More than 3,500 people lived there in 1900. (Denver Public Library Western Collection)

Independence in 1900. Two thousand people lived there. (Denver Public Library Western Collection)

When this picture was taken, Altman had a population of 1,500. At 10,620 feet, it was the highest incorporated city in the world. Pikes Peak is in the background. (Denver Public Library Western Collection)

Miner's homes in Anaconda. It once had a population of about 1,500. (Denver Public Library Western Collection)

Gillett, in 1900, had a population of about 1,200. This was its Main Street. (State Historical Society of Colorado)

The Gillett bullring, built in 1895, held 5,000. It stood in Sportsman Park, the camp's racetrack One of the nation's few bullfights was staged there. (Denver Public Library Western Collection)

LIFE IN THE GOLD CAMP

Except for their early days, Cripple Creek and Victor were more than just mining camps. They quickly grew into modern cities, and for the most part, life there for the average person was about the same as it was in any other modern turn-of-the-century city.

On a Sunday morning, thousands of persons crowded into the District's thirty-four churches. There were sixteen in Cripple Creek alone, and Victor had about half as many. The camp's smaller towns had two or three churches each.

The Teller County School System had an excellent reputation. The following story was seen in a special 1903 edition of the *Cripple Creek Times:*

> "— It may surprise the people of the plains to know that this mining camp spends more money on the education of her youth than any community in the land of like size."

At that time, 3,849 students were enrolled in the District's nineteen schools, and 118 teachers were employed. Cripple Creek and Victor both had high schools. The one in Cripple Creek offered night classes to the adult population as early as 1896.

During the camp's heyday, there were eighty-three lodges representing thirty-eight different orders. There were scores of clubs and organizations including a medical society, bar association, press club and pharmacists' association. More than 100 women's clubs met regularly.

During the early 1900's, the District was the stronghold of organized labor in Colorado. Every Labor Day, in a show of great strength, many thousands of union workers marched up the main streets of the two cities. Included were members of the cigar makers, tailors, stage employees, waiters, signwriters and, of course, mining unions.

The community's cultural life centered around the opera houses. There were two in Cripple Creek, and another in Victor. Each seated between 800 and 1,000 people. Admissions to their stage attractions ran from 15 cents to a top of 35 cents.

During a single week in the spring of 1900, the Grand Opera House in Cripple Creek presented Miss Leonora Jackson in a violin concert, a hit play, two performances by the Lombardi Grand Opera Company and a production of "Uncle Tom's Cabin."

Regarding the play, the *Cripple Creek Times* reported:

> "The District's society people enjoyed a great treat at the Grand Opera House Monday night, when Blanch Walsh and her New York Company presented 'More than a Queen'. Victor's social set was well represented with two special trains bringing them over."

Then in only a few days, the *Times* announced another show:

> "This Sunday evening, the Dobbins Brothers big production of 'Uncle Tom's Cabin' will hold the boards at the Grand. Be sure to see the big parade at noon on Sunday with two bands, ten Shetland ponies, bloodhounds, floats and gorgeous banners."

Cripple Creek also had a vaudeville theatre called the Crystal. On the top circuits, it presented three shows every night and two matinees a week.

The District's theatres and opera houses were also used for political rallies, revival meetings and sports events. The world's first indoor rodeo was staged at the Grand, and this was where the big prize fights were held.

A good fight bill brought out as many as 2,000 fans, coming from as far away as Denver, to see such fighters as Jack Dempsey and Jack Johnson.

Baseball games attracted even bigger crowds. As many as 5,000 people packed into Cripple Creek's Union Park for some games.

Then there was the summer racing season at Gillett's Sportsman Park. On a single afternoon, as many as 3,000 race fans turned out to see the West's finest horses in action. Special trains brought them to the track from Cripple Creek and Victor.

The nation's big tent shows and circuses played Cripple Creek as early as 1896. They came in their own trains and promoted their shows with long and colorful parades.

During the long winter months, both Cripple Creek and Victor had lighted skating rinks. Cripple Creek always opened hers with the annual Elks Club Winter Carnival.

If there was one red letter day a year in the District, it was the Fourth of July. On that day in 1900, Cripple Creek celebrated with a parade that was eighteen blocks long. Over 10,000 people lined Bennett Avenue to see it!

Cripple Creek's first church. By 1900, there were thirty-four church buildings in the mining camp. (State Historical Society of Colorado)

The school house at Anaconda was one of nineteen which served the District during the boom. (Denver Public Library Western Collection)

Thousands celebrated the Fourth of July in Cripple Creek every year. This 1898 crowd is watching a hose race up the city's main street.

Victor, July 4, 1895. The holiday crowd is seen in front of the old Victor Hotel.

The Knights of Pythias on parade in downtown Victor. There were eighty-three lodges in the District during its heyday. (State Historical Society of Colorado)

A matinee audience at Cripple Creek's Butte Opera House, July 7, 1895. (Imperial Hotel Collection)

Looking east on Bennett Avenue, Cripple Creek's unique two-level street. The town was decorated for a lodge convention.

Yes, it snows in Cripple Creek! This huge drift almost blocked Bennett Avenue in front of the First National Bank building. Heavy snows have fallen as late as June 9 and as early as Labor Day.

THE MINES

In 1900, gold worth more than $18,000,000 was mined in the Cripple Creek District. That was the peak year. Then almost 500 mines were operating with some 8,000 miners creating a monthly payroll of $900,000.

The Portland Mine, alone, employed 700 men and worked them in three eight-hour shifts. For a short time, Jack Dempsey was on the Portland's payroll.

Of the District's mines, the Portland was the largest and the richest. Over a fifty-year period, it produced gold worth over $60,000,000. Standing on Battle Mountain, just above Victor, the Portland's buildings and dumps sprawled over 180 acres. Its 3,200-foot shaft was the deepest in the camp.

The Cresson, halfway between Victor and Cripple Creek, was the District's second greatest producer. In 1914, the field's richest discovery was made there. A small cavity on the 1,200-foot level produced four carloads of ore worth almost $500,000. Some of it was worth as much as $50 a pound!

The Cresson's "treasure chest" was locked off from the other parts of the mine with a vault door. Armed guards stood by while it was worked out. The ore left the mine in locked boxcars and guards stayed on the train until it reached the mill in Colorado City.

Cripple Creek gold produced thirty millionaires. Winfield Scott Stratton, a Colorado Springs carpenter, was the first. After fifteen years of prospecting, he struck paydirt on July 4, 1891, and called his claim the Independence.

Stratton took over $4,000,000 out of his mine before selling it to a London Company for $11,000,000. The Independence ultimately produced more than $28,000,000 worth of gold.

One of the Gold Camp's principal mines was located right in the very heart of downtown Victor. While land there was being leveled off for a hotel building, rich ore was discovered. The hotel plans were junked on the spot, and the great Gold Coin Mine came into being.

The Pharmacist Mine in Altman was also discovered by pure chance. Not knowing where to start digging, the druggist who made this strike, threw his hat in the air. He dug where it fell, hit a rich vein and became one of the District's millionaires.

The Cash-On-Delivery Mine in Poverty Gulch gave Spencer Penrose his first great wealth. Penrose's C.O.D. profits were wisely invested in milling and other mining enterprises, and in 1918, he built the Broadmoor Hotel in Colorado Springs.

Other of the District's better known mines included the Elkton, Ajax, Golden Cycle, Anchoria Leland, Gold King, Strong, El Paso and Isabella. And there was the Moon Anchor, Christmas, War Eagle, Ocean Wave, Wild Horse, Joe Dandy, Conundrum, and Sitting Bull; 500 mines with 500 names!

Cripple Creek was known as a "Three Dollar Camp" because no miner was paid less than that for his day's work. However, by "high-grading," most men made a good deal more.

"High-grading" was the stealing of the very richest ore. The miners carried it out in their lunch buckets, pants cuffs, hats and pockets. There was always a ready market for "high-grade" ore in Cripple Creek and Victor.

Gold mine stocks were traded at the Cripple Creek Stock Exchange as well as at the Colorado Springs Exchange pictured here.

Deep in the Half Moon Mine. Over 8,000 men were employed by Cripple Creek's gold mines in 1900. (Denver Public Library Western Collection)

Not all the 350 employees of the Gold Coin Mine worked in the mine. Some worked on the surface in the ore house.

The great mines of Battle Mountain above Victor produced gold worth well over $125,000,000. The Portland, Independence, Strong, and Ajax were all located here. (Denver Public Library Western Collection)

Surface buildings of the rich El Paso Mine, halfway between Cripple Creek and Victor. Deeper than the Empire State Building is high, the El Paso has over thirty-three miles of railed underground diggings.

As late as 1938, the Cresson Mine worked well over 100 men. (John Abel Collection)

Lunch time at the Dr. Jackpot. Its rich ore was shipped out in locked box cars.

The C.O.D. Mine in Poverty Gulch near Womack's original discovery helped to establish the fortune that built the Broadmoor Hotel in Colorado Springs. (Broadmoor Hotel Collection)

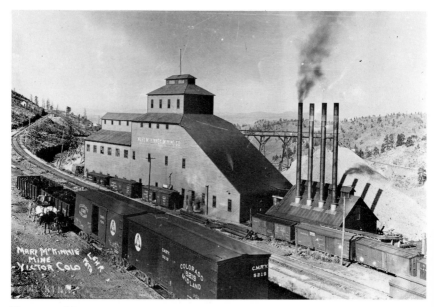

The present Mary McKinney Mine at Anaconda.

The great Cresson Mine in Eclipse Gulch produced more than $50,000,000 worth of gold. (John Abel Collection)

This was the Vindicator. It stood above Independence at an elevation of 10,210 feet.

The Eagle Sampler Gold Mine was served by four levels of railroad tracks. One passed directly through the ore house.

RAILROADS

At the turn of the century, the gold camp was served by three different railroads and two electric interurban systems. As many as fifty-eight passenger trains a day arrived at Cripple Creek's stations!

The District's first train arrived on July 1, 1894. This was the narrow gauge Florence and Cripple Creek Railroad. It steamed up Phantom Canyon from Florence to Victor and then through Elkton and Anaconda to Cripple Creek — a climb of about 5,000 feet over forty miles of steep, winding grades.

Known as "The Gold Belt Line," the Florence and Cripple Creek ran three passenger trains each way on a daily schedule between Florence and Cripple Creek. Slender little Pullman cars left Cripple Creek every night at nine o'clock to arrive in Denver early the next morning. At one-thirty every morning another Pullman train left Colorado Springs for the Gold Camp. It was called "The Cripple Creek Special."

Business was good. The Florence and Cripple Creek paid for itself the very first year it operated. The line continued to run until 1912, when a flood in Phantom Canyon washed out much of the road.

The second railroad into the District was the standard gauge Midland Terminal. It served Cripple Creek for over half a century, starting in December, 1895.

The Midland Terminal traveled up Ute Pass over the Colorado Midland Road from Colorado Springs to Divide. There it struck off south into rugged mountain country to Gillett. From there, it continued on to Cameron, over 10,260-foot Victor Pass, through Independence to Victor. Then it passed through Elkton and Anaconda before reaching the big three-story brick depot at the end of Bennett Avenue in Cripple Creek.

It was fifty-five miles to Cripple Creek from Colorado Springs by way of the Midland Terminal. The trip took a little over two hours. A round trip coach ticket cost $2.50.

The Midland Terminal operated four trains a day to and from Cripple Creek. Passengers for the District could leave Colorado Springs every morning at three-thirty, eight-thirty-five, or eleven-fifteen. Or they could take the evening train. Trains left Cripple Creek for Colorado Springs every morning at two-forty and every afternoon at two-twenty-five, six-thirty or eight-fifteen. The "Cripple Creek Flyer" provided Pullman service between the two cities.

As long as the District's ore had to be hauled to the processing mill in Colorado Springs, the Midland Terminal held on as a freight line. But the building of the new Carlton Mill near Victor in 1949, eliminated any need for a rail line, so that year, the Midland Terminal passed from the scene.

It was five years after the arrival of the Midland Terminal before the third line pushed up from Colorado Springs to the District. It was named The Colorado Springs and Cripple Creek District Railroad, but better known as "The Short Line." Starting on April 12, 1901, it operated two passenger trains a day each way over standard gauge tracks.

This was the most direct and the most scenic route into the Cripple Creek area. For "The Short Line" headed right out over the hills from Colorado Springs for the District. Heralded from the start as a marvel of railroad engineering, the forty-five-mile line fast became one of the West's greatest tourist attractions, serving the District until 1920.

Besides the fast and frequent passenger trains that operated within the District, there were two electric trolley systems. They provided day and night service to all the cities in the camp and to the principal mines.

The High Line Electric made a six-mile run between Cripple Creek and Victor by way of Midway. At one point, it reached an elevation of 10,487 feet.

The Low Line Electric also connected the camp's two big towns and served Elkton and Anaconda. Trains ran every thirty minutes over this road. The fare was five cents.

Both trolley systems halted operation in 1922.

After the railroads were dismantled, most of the old grades were converted into auto highways. The Florence and Cripple Creek road became the Phantom Canyon auto highway. The Gold Camp Road was built over what had been the Short Line. And, Colorado State Highway 67 uses several miles of old Midland Terminal grades between Divide and Gillett.

The Florence and Cripple Creek depot in Cripple Creek.

Gillett was the "gateway" to the District. This was the Midland Terminal depot there. (Denver Public Library Western Collection)

The first rail service into the District was over the narrow gauge Florence and Cripple Creek line. These steep grades were just south of Victor. (Denver Public Library Western Collection)

A train load of gold ore heading for the mill in Colorado City over Midland Terminal rails.

The Midland Terminal Railroad approached the Cripple Creek depot over Poverty Gulch near the spot where Bob Womack discovered gold. (Denver Public Library Western Collection)

The last train out of Cripple Creek. After serving the District for half a century. The Midland Terminal stopped operating in 1949. (Denver Public Library Western Collection. Photo by Ernest Peyton)

This is a Short Line passenger train about halfway between Victor and Cripple Creek. The Sangre de Cristo Mountains can be seen in the background.

The District yards for the Florence and Cripple Creek were just below the Strong Mine in Victor.

For almost twenty-five years, the cities of the Cripple Creek District were linked together by two electric interurban systems. This early drawing shows their routes. (Denver Public Library Western Collection)

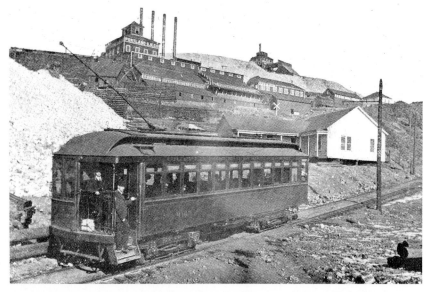

The electric trains made regular stops at all the leading mines. This is a High Line car at the Portland. Pioneer's Museum, Colorado Springs)

RED LIGHTS

"There'll be a Hot Time in the Old Town Tonight" was first heard on Myers Avenue in Cripple Creek. And it fit, for this was one of the largest and most boisterous of the Old West's red-light districts.

Between Third Street and where it played out at the mouth of Poverty Gulch, Myers Avenue was lined with variety theatres, dance halls, saloons, gambling halls, parlour houses and cribs. It churned twenty-four hours a day with free-spending miners who were out for a good time.

There were two schools of thought on Cripple Creek's red-light district. Some argued that the "tenderloin" made it safe for the District's "decent" women to walk on the streets. A Cripple Creek Baptist minister was one who saw no good at all in the shabby section. One Sunday morning, he told his congregation:

> "It is disgraceful that our street cars must pass down Myers Avenue, where a decent woman is ashamed to be seen. Whenever I pass through that district in one of the cars, I make a monkey out of myself to keep the people's attention off the street's shocking sights."

The "shows" within the variety theatres were even more shocking. To drum up business, the managements of Crapper Jack's, The Red Light, The Bon Ton and other places sent their bands out to parade up and down the Avenue just before show-time.

One of Myers Avenue's saloons was a huge German beer garden where miners were served schooners of beer while being entertained by an honest-to-goodness German band. Then there was the Opera Club, Old Yellowstone, Swanee River, Last Chance, the Abbey, Miner's Exchange and one called the Dawson Club. A shooting took place there one night and it was reported this way by the *Cripple Creek Times*:

> "An inquest was held at Lampman's morgue today over the body of James S. F. Roberts who was shot last night at the Dawson Club on Myers Avenue. Thirteen witnesses testified. They were comprised of girls of the half-world, the Dawson Club piano player, the bartender and members of the police force. One of the witnesses said that as the man lay on the floor dying some of the crowd urged him to the bar for a drink."

In the alleys behind the Myers Avenue joints, there were several opium dens. These 1900 newspaper stories tell of still another kind of life the red-light district knew then:

> " 'A hop joint' in the small brick building behind the Red Light Dance hall was raided at noon today. The room was elaborately outfitted. The accounts kept show that the den was well patronized by people of Myers Avenue."

> "Another opium den was raided yesterday. The police, for several days, have been watching the apartment of Lizzie Moore. Yesterday, the captain noticed three women go there at 6:00 a.m. After a quarter of an hour, the captain tiptoed in to find the women and the proprietress reclining on a Turkish rug, hitting the pipe."

While there were many "houses" on Myers Avenue during the boom, it was the Old Homestead at 353 that always enjoyed the finest clientele of any brothel in the gold camp. From the day it opened, this posh house was the playground of the mining kings.

Others had to find their pleasures in the less elegant places on "the row." There were plenty to choose from. In 1900, in the same block with the Old Homestead, there were four others — Laura Bell's, the Mikado, Nell McClusky's, and the Royal Inn. The Boston was a block away on Myers and the Parisian was on Fifth Street.

In addition to the fancy houses, there were scores of one-girl cribs. Most of them were strung out in Poverty Gulch for about a quarter of a mile. The cribs represented a progression of races. First, there were French girls, then Japanese, Chinese, Mexican and Negro.

The cribs were flimsy two-room affairs that fronted right on the dirt street. Each had a narrow door and tiny window. The crib girls solicited from their front doors. The shacks they lived in were identified with their names: Kitty, Eva, Dolly, Frankie, Doe, Dot, painted on the crib's door.

There was still some life on "the row" as late as 1914. That was the year Julian Street was in Cripple Creek to get material for a travel series he was writing for *Collier's Weekly Magazine*. When the story appeared, the people of Cripple Creek were furious, for Street wrote about nothing but the shabby red-light district and its few sordid inhabitants.

Some weeks later, Cripple Creek "honored" the writer by officially changing the name of Myers Avenue to Julian Street.

There were 150 saloons in the District in 1900. Seventy-three of them were in Cripple Creek. Most of them faced Myers Avenue, the big town's "sin street." (Denver Public Library Western Collection)

"The Row" in early Cripple Creek. Beyond the "houses," a few one-girl cribs can be seen. (Denver Public Library Western Collection. Photo by H. S. Poley)

When Pearl DeVere, madame of the Old Homestead, died in 1897, her body was accompanied to Mt. Pisgah Cemetery by four mounted police officers, a twenty-piece Elks Club band and a dozen buggies filled with girls from "the row." (Photo by Ted S. McKee)

The arrow points to the Old Homestead, center of Cripple Creek's notorious red-light district. The Grand Opera House can be seen on the opposite side of the street. (Fred and Jo Mazzulla Collection)

END OF AN ERA

After 1900, the District's production and population both began to decline.

The first cause was the labor war which lasted for a year and a half and claimed thirty-three lives. It was called in August of 1903, by the Western Federation of Miners over a Colorado City mill workers' dispute. The strike idled 3,550 men and brought about the complete collapse of organized labor in the gold camp.

After the labor problems had been worked out, a long period of consolidation began. The mergers eliminated jobs and forced many out of the District.

Then water trouble developed. Pumping it up out of mines that were as deep as 3,000 feet proved too expensive. There was only one thing to do; drain the whole mining district.

In 1911, the three-mile Roosevelt Tunnel was bored back into the gold field. It lowered the water level in many mines and increased production. Thirty years later, the six-mile Carlton Tunnel drained the District still deeper.

About 150 mines continued shipping ore until World War I closed them. By 1920, only forty mines were operating, with their annual production down to $4,000,000. In another ten years, it was down to about $2,500,000.

The District experienced quite a boom when, in 1934, the price of gold was increased to $35 an ounce. Many mines reopened. By 1936, 135 of them were shipping ore once again, and production was back up to more than $5,000,000 a year.

When World War II began, 100 Cripple Creek mines were operating. But by 1945, less than twenty were being worked, and, for the first time since the year of the discovery, production slipped to under $1,000,000.

There was some flurry of activity right after the war, but it was in 1951, that the District experienced the last suggestion of a "boom." Then the Carlton Mill was opened near Victor. Thirty mines produced more than $2,000,000 worth of gold that year.

The new mill operated until 1962, and a few mines worked as late as 1961. They did not close for a lack of good ore. It simply cannot be mined profitably at today's high production costs.

Bennett Avenue after a heavy snow in 1920.

Violence often erupted on the streets of Cripple Creek in 1903 and 1904 while one of Colorado's most serious labor wars raged. This mob is pictured in front of the Gold Mining Exchange Building. (Denver Public Library Western Collection)

During the long and bloody labor war, the District was occupied by the Colorado National Guard. This was Camp Goldfield on Battle Mountain just above Goldfield and Victor. (Denver Public Library Western Collection)

"The Towers" was the finest home ever built in Cripple Creek. The twenty-six room mansion was the home of J. Maurice Finn, an attorney. Teddy Roosevelt was entertained there in 1901. It was razed in 1920.

By 1921, Cripple Creek had begun to look deserted. The District's population, by then, had slipped to about 5,000. (State Historical Society of Colorado)

Cripple Creek's museum was once the Midland Terminal Railroad station. More than 100,000 tourists now visit it each summer. (Colorado Springs Chamber of Commerce)

Tourists, not miners, now crowd the streets of old Cripple Creek.

TODAY

Fewer than 1,000 people live in the District now. Cripple Creek's permanent population has shrunk to 600 and Victor's to about 250.

But each summer, the District is invaded by bigger and bigger numbers of tourists and summer residents. Gold mining, then, has been replaced by tourism as the leading industry.

Cripple Creek and Victor have excellent museums. The Mollie Kathleen Mine is open to visitors. The thrill of steam railroading can be experienced again on the Cripple Creek and Victor Narrow Gauge. And there is the scenic spiral drive to the top of 10,400 foot Mt. Pisgah. But the biggest attraction is the Melodrama at the Imperial Hotel.

Dorothy and Wayne Mackin, an imaginative and energetic couple, bought and reopened the old Cripple Creek hotel in 1946, and presented their first melodrama in 1947. The following year, they opened the now famous Gold Bar Room Theatre in the Imperial's basement.

That season, the Imperial entertained about 4,500 guests. Now well over 35,000 people enjoy the authentic Victorian dramas each summer in the beautifully restored old Imperial.

Cripple Creek today. (Photo courtesy Magic Lantern Theatre)

Cripple Creek's Imperial Hotel, built in 1896, was bought and reopened in 1946, by Dorothy and Wayne Mackin who have since developed it into the nationally known melodrama theatre. (Imperial Hotel Collection)

The Cripple Creek Travel Park and Hospitality House, another Mackin development, was once the Teller County Hospital. The old building offers attractive overnight accommodations and the park surround it provides space for campers. (Imperial Hotel Collection)

Many of the District's fine old Victorian houses have been restored in recent years for summer homes.

The Teller County Courthouse, built in 1904 at a cost of $60,000, is still in use.

Cripple Creek now. The white building is the Old Homestead Parlour House. It stands alone on Myers Avenue. (Photo by Tom Harrington)

Looking up Third Street in Cripple Creek. It was once the route of the street cars.

Victor today. Once a city of over 18,000 people, only about 250 live there now. (Photo by Tom Harrington)

The little one story building on Victor's Fourth Street housed The Victor Record, where Lowell Thomas began his career.

Goldfield's city hall and fire station. Once a city of 3,500, the population now is less than twenty.

When Elkton was a city of 2,500, it had a thriving business district. This was one of the grocery stores.

A few buildings at Anaconda, once a town of some 1,500. (Photo by Roger Appleton)

The saloon at Midway. At 10,487 feet, Midway was the highest point in the District to be reached by street cars.

Area pioneers are buried in the District's two cemeteries, Mt. Pisgah at Cripple Creek and in Victor's Sunnyside.

Stratton's fabulous Independence Mine as it looks today.

Two burros of Cripple Creek lunching in what was once Union Park, the city's baseball field. (Photo by Terry Skelton)

Once again, a cow pasture.

The Carlton Mill, midway between Victor and Cripple Creek, is the largest custom gold mill in the world. (Photo by Maxine Adams)

TOMORROW

While the Cripple Creek area continues to boom as a tourist center, with many new shops and attractions there are strong indications the District is going to become an active gold mining center once again!

Recently Cripple Creek Gold Corporation, a subsidiary firm of the Golden Cycle Corporation announced plans for a $6,000,000 project over the next three years which will see the reopening of the Ajax Mine on Battle Mountain above Victor.

The Company claims the mining reactivation project will eventually employ between 50 and 100 men. The old Carlton Mill, quiet since 1962, will be rehabilitated or a new mill will be built in that area to process the District's gold output.

The Ajax Mine on Battle Mountain may soon be a working mine once again. The now deserted Victor High School Building stands in the foreground.

Victor's old houses have begun filling with miners and their families again. The arrow points to the house in which Lowell Thomas lived as a child.

BIBLIOGRAPHY

For those who want to read about the Cripple Creek District in more depth, these books are recommended:

Cafky, Morris, *Rails Around Gold Hill.* Rocky Mountain Railroad Club. 1955

Dorset, Phyllis Flanders, *The New Eldorado.* MacMillan. 1970

Eberhart, Perry, *Guide to Colorado Ghost Towns and Mining Camps.* Sage Books. 1959

Ellis, Amanda, *Bonanza Towns.* Dentan. 1954

Ellis, Amanda, *Those Strange Uncertain Years.* Shoe String Press. 1959

Feitz, Leland, *Myers Avenue.* Little London Press. 1967

Feitz, Leland, *Cripple Creek Railroads.* Little London Press. 1969

Feitz, Leland, *Victor, Colorado's City of Mines.* Little London Press. 1969

Feitz, Leland, *Ghost Towns of the Cripple Creek District.* Little London Press. 1975

Hafen & Hafen, *Colorado.* Old West. 1953

Lee, Mable Barbee, *Cripple Creek Days.* Doubleday. 1958

Lee, Mable Barbee, *Back in Cripple Creek.* Doubleday. 1968

Lipsey, John J., *The Lives of John J. Hagerman.* Golden Bell. 1968

Mazzula, Fred & Jo, *The First 100 Years.* 1956

Spraque, Marshall, *Money Mountain.* Little Brown & Co. 1957

Spraque, Marshall, *Newport in the Rockies.* Sage Books. 1971

Taylor, Robert Guilford, *Cripple Creek.* University of Indiana. 1966

Waters, Frank, *Midas of the Rockies.* Sage Books. 1937

Wolle, Muriel Sibell, *Stampede to Timberline.* Sage Books. 1949

Mt. Pisgah. The view of the mining district from its summit is magnificent. A road spirals to the top.